Worldwide Wonders

MAN-MADE WONDERS

Clive Gifford

WAYLAND
www.waylandbooks.co.uk

Published in paperpack in Great Britain in 2018 by Wayland

Editor: Nicola Edwards
Design: Peter Clayman

ISBN: 978 0 7502 9868 1
10 9 8 7 6 5 4 3 2 1

MIX
Paper from
responsible sources
FSC® C104740

Wayland, an imprint of
Hachette Children's Group
Part of Hodder and Stoughton
Carmelite House
50 Victoria Embankment
London EC4Y 0DZ

An Hachette UK Company
www.hachette.co.uk
www.hachettechildrens.co.uk

Printed and bound in China

Picture acknowledgements: All images and graphic elements courtesy of Shutterstock
except p9t, p10t, p13t, p14b, p17t Getty images; p23 (t and m) Corbis; p23b Getty
images; p26 Maximilien Brice, CERN; p27 (t and b) CERN.

Every attempt has been made to clear copyright. Should there be any
inadvertent omission, please apply to the publisher for rectification.

The website addresses (URLs) included in this book were valid at the time of
going to press. However, it is possible that contents or addresses may have
changed since the publication of this book. No responsibility for any such
changes can be accepted by either the author or the Publisher.

Contents

The Empire State Building

This book is all about the astonishing and groundbreaking buildings, bridges and other structures people have created that have become wonders of the world. Among them is perhaps the most famous skyscraper of them all, the Empire State Building on Fifth Avenue in the US city of New York.

Race to the Skies

In the early part of the twentieth century, a race began among wealthy US businessmen to produce the tallest buildings in America. A consortium of investors decided the site of the former Waldorf-Astoria Hotel, demolished in 1929, would beat all rivals. Construction began on 17 March 1930. A large team of some 3,400 workers erected the Building at a lightning-fast rate of around four and a half storeys per week. By 1 May 1931, the entire 102 storey building was complete. Towering 381m over the centre of Manhattan, it was the tallest building in the world until 1972. Today, with its mast containing a television antenna spire and a lightning conductor, it stands 443m high.

In 2009, US$550 million was spent on renovations, including new windows.

The Empire State Building towers over its neighbours in Manhattan.

Inside and Out

The Empire State Building was constructed from a framework of over 55,000 tonnes of steel. Around the building's 6,500 windows were aluminium panels, and some 10 million bricks were used to line the building. The whole structure is supported on more than 200 concrete and steel piles. Inside, 73 elevators ferry people up and down the building at a top speed of 7.1m per second. Around 21,000 people work in offices throughout the building, making it one of the most populated office blocks in the world.

The building's lobby is a preserved historic landmark.

WOW!

There are 1,576 steps from the ground to the 86th floor observation deck. The Empire State Run-Up race sees who can complete the journey in the shortest time. The record stands at a lung-busting 9 minutes, 33 seconds.

Visitors can enjoy amazing views of New York.

Great Views

After a rocky start when it was nicknamed the Empty State Building because of the difficulty in getting businesses to rent office space, the skyscraper has become an extremely popular American icon. Some four million people visit every year, and many travel to the two observation decks on the 86th and 102nd floors. The 86th floor observation deck gives visitors incredible 360-degree views of New York and beyond, while visibility from the 102nd floor deck can be up to 125km on a clear day.

The Taj Mahal

Mughal emperor Shah Jahan ordered the construction of a magnificent mausoleum to house the tomb of his beloved wife, Mumtaz Mahal in 1631. The result is one of Asia's most spectacular and beautiful buildings, which attracts millions of visitors every year.

Perched on the banks of the Yamuna River near the city of Agra, the Taj Mahal is set within a 300-metre-square garden called a charbagh made of raised pathways and sunken flowerbeds. In the garden, a canal and 24 fountains are fed by an elaborate system of waterworks. A large rectangular pond, the Lotus Pool, stands in front of the canal and the still waters reflect the Taj Mahal.

WOW!

A giant scaffold made of brick surrounded the Taj Mahal during its construction. Another set of scaffolding covered the building again during World War II to protect it from attack by enemy aircraft.

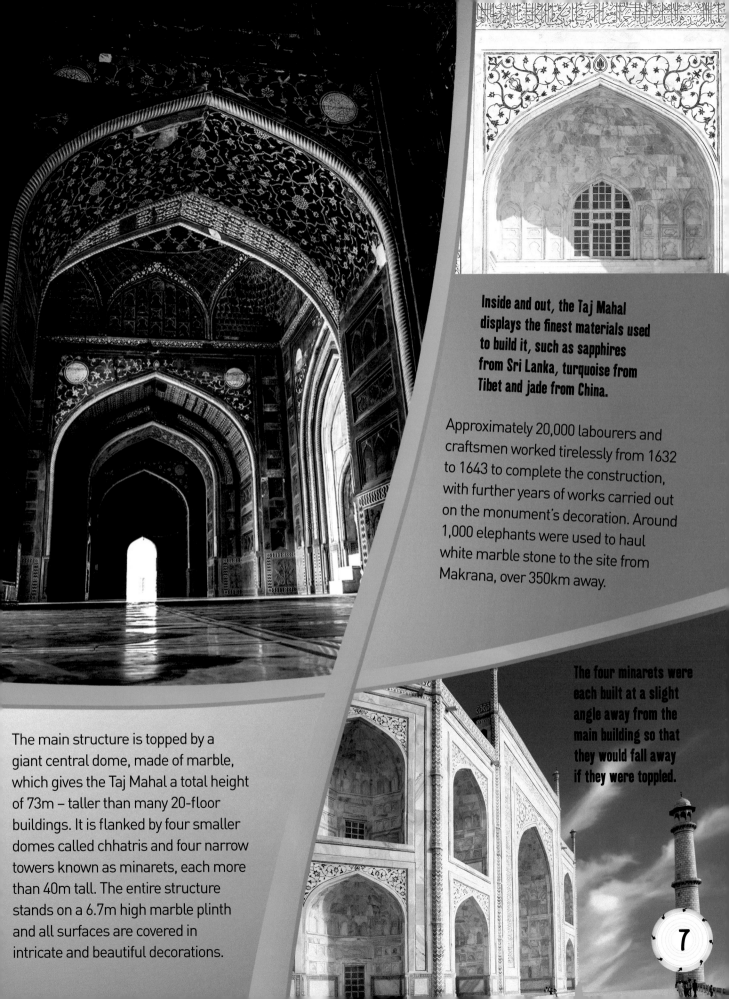

Inside and out, the Taj Mahal displays the finest materials used to build it, such as sapphires from Sri Lanka, turquoise from Tibet and jade from China.

Approximately 20,000 labourers and craftsmen worked tirelessly from 1632 to 1643 to complete the construction, with further years of works carried out on the monument's decoration. Around 1,000 elephants were used to haul white marble stone to the site from Makrana, over 350km away.

The four minarets were each built at a slight angle away from the main building so that they would fall away if they were toppled.

The main structure is topped by a giant central dome, made of marble, which gives the Taj Mahal a total height of 73m – taller than many 20-floor buildings. It is flanked by four smaller domes called chhatris and four narrow towers known as minarets, each more than 40m tall. The entire structure stands on a 6.7m high marble plinth and all surfaces are covered in intricate and beautiful decorations.

The Millau Viaduct

Traffic congestion on a stretch of the A75 road – part of the major route between Paris and southern France and Spain – led the authorities to consider ways to bypass a 25km stretch of road along the Tarn Valley. The resulting solution, the Millau Viaduct, not only slashed journey times from as much as three hours to just 20 minutes, but also created an exciting and elegant symbol of modern France.

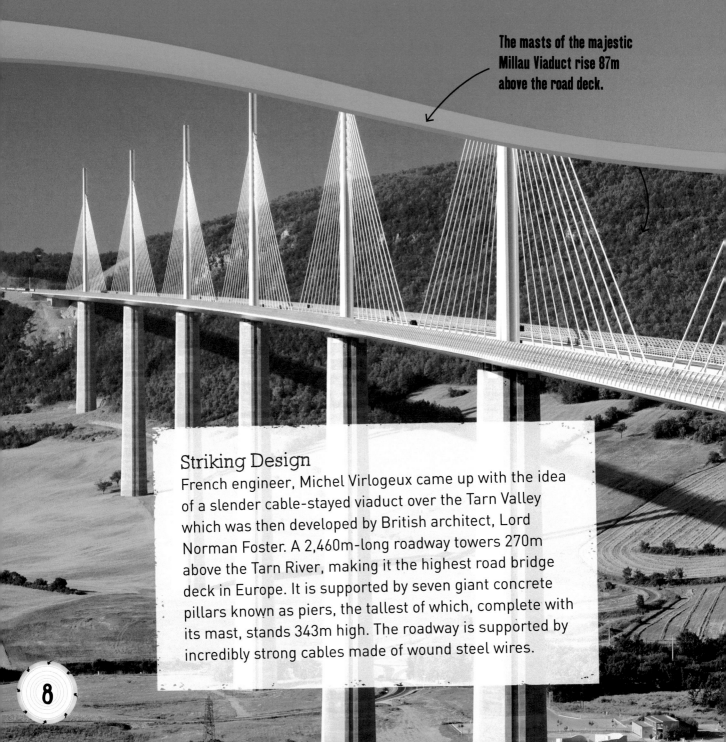

The masts of the majestic Millau Viaduct rise 87m above the road deck.

Striking Design

French engineer, Michel Virlogeux came up with the idea of a slender cable-stayed viaduct over the Tarn Valley which was then developed by British architect, Lord Norman Foster. A 2,460m-long roadway towers 270m above the Tarn River, making it the highest road bridge deck in Europe. It is supported by seven giant concrete pillars known as piers, the tallest of which, complete with its mast, stands 343m high. The roadway is supported by incredibly strong cables made of wound steel wires.

Bridge Building

Construction began in December 2001 with the digging of the foundations for the giant piers. It took just three years for the structure to be completed and opened, an astonishing feat of engineering. Some 85,000 cubic metres of concrete was used to create the bridge, which weighs 290,000 tonnes. Around 15,000-20,000 vehicles cross it every day, each paying a toll to make the journey.

Some 19,000 tonnes of steel were used to reinforce the concrete during construction.

The road deck weighs 36,000 tonnes and is 4.2m thick and 32m wide, with room for four lanes of traffic.

Viaduct Visitors

Apart from regular road traffic, many people make detours from their routes through southern France to view the viaduct at close quarters. A popular pursuit is to canoe under the viaduct along the Tarn River. The Viaduc Espace Info visitor centre at the base of the viaduct offers an Explorers Garden – an open air exhibition about the viaduct and its construction – as well as entry inside part of the P2 pillar, the tallest bridge or viaduct pillar in the world.

WOW!

To monitor the structure's safety, 12 sensors fitted into the P2 pillar measure the stresses and force the pillar is under as often as 100 times every second.

The Sydney Opera House

The Sydney Opera House opened in 1973, after 14 years of construction. Its daring design has made it an international icon. Visited by around two million people every year, it remains one of the most distinctive buildings in the world, with giant concrete sails forming its famous roof.

Competition Winner

A competition for a new concert and arts venue in Australia's biggest city attracted 233 entries from architects hailing from 32 different countries. The entry of Denmark's Jorn Utzon was originally rejected by three of the judges before a fourth, Eero Saarinen, swayed opinion. Construction of Utzon's design began in 1959, with 580 piers sunk into the ground to support the building's great weight – 161,000 tonnes or 789 times the weight of the Statue of Liberty.

Concrete and Ceramics

Built to face Sydney Harbour on the site of a demolished tram depot, the Sydney Opera House is approximately 183m long and 120m wide at its widest point. It is made up of a large number of different-sized rooms and venues, all topped by a giant roof which stands 67m above the ground at its highest point. The roof was made of 2,194 separate sections of pre-cast concrete which were fitted together using special-purpose cranes shipped over from France. The roof is covered in a staggering 1.05 million dazzling ceramic tiles from Sweden.

WOW!

A staggering 15,500 light bulbs are replaced on average every year within the Sydney Opera House. The building uses as much electricity as a town holding up to 25,000 people!

The ceramic tiles were bonded to more than 4,000 panels which were then bolted to the concrete roof shells.

Not Only Opera

Despite its name, the building hosts all types of arts, theatre and music performances, around 3,000 different events each year. These are held in its seven indoor venues including the 2,679-seat Concert Hall, which is home to a gigantic mechanical pipe organ with 10,154 pipes. There's also an outdoor forecourt area for performances in front of as many as 6,000 people, as well as a recording studio, restaurants, cafes, bars and other facilities.

Mount Rushmore

Looming over the more than two million visitors who come to Dakota's Black Hills every year, are the giant faces of four celebrated presidents of the United States. This remarkable sculpture is hewn into the granite rock of the south-eastern face of Mount Rushmore near the town of Keystone in South Dakota.

Left to right, Mount Rushmore depicts the faces of George Washington, Thomas Jefferson, Theodore Roosevelt and Abraham Lincoln. Each of the eyes is 3.35m wide!

Off the Drawing Board

In 1923, a local historian, Doane Robinson, was the first to put forward the idea of creating a giant sculpture in the state's Black Hills. He suggested it should commemorate famous American folk heroes and Native American leaders. However its sculptor, Gutzon Borglum, decided it would portray four US presidents – George Washington as the first president, Abraham Lincoln for his leadership during the US Civil War, Thomas Jefferson for his role in expanding the country and popular early-20th-century president, Theodore Roosevelt.

Blast Off!

Work began in 1927 and continued for 14 years. The rock face had to be blasted off with mining explosives then chipped away at using jackhammers (pneumatic drills) before being hand drilled, chiselled and smoothed to create the faces. Over 400,000 tonnes of rock was removed in this way by around 400 workers. Borglum died in 1941 but his son, Lincoln, continued the work which was halted later that year. The resulting sculptures stand 18m tall, the same size as many six-storey buildings.

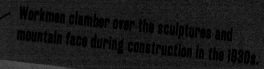

Workmen clamber over the sculptures and mountain face during construction in the 1930s.

WOW!

Thomas Jefferson's head was originally carved to George Washington's right. When a large crack was found in the rock beneath it, the face was dynamited off the rock and carved again, but this time on Washington's left-hand side.

Monitoring and Preservation

A 10-year modernisation plan completed walkways, a museum and visitor centre which opened in 1998. In the same year a laser monitoring system was fitted to the monument to detect any cracks or shifts in the rock. The US National Park Service employs mountain climbers to seal any cracks they find using a silicon sealant disguised with granite dust to fit in with the surrounding rock. In 2005, the entire sculpture received a steam clean courtesy of a German pressure cleaner company to remove lichens and moss from the rock.

The Three Gorges Dam

The world's biggest dam is a barrier across Asia's longest river, the Yangtze, in China's Hubei Province. The Yangtze has flooded disastrously in the past and the dam was designed to help control the river's water flow as well as to generate huge amounts of electricity. Its design has also allowed large ocean-going cargo ships to travel further inland than before. Ships can now sail over 2,000km inland from the major city of Shanghai on China's eastern coast.

Supersized Structure

Work began in 1994 and continued through to 2012, although the main body of the dam was largely finished by 2006. It is an absolutely enormous structure, 2,335m long and 185m high at its highest point – as tall as many 60-storey buildings. It was built mostly from vast quantities of concrete reinforced with enough steel to build more than 60 Eiffel Towers (see pages 20-21). Behind the dam, lies a giant, 600km-long reservoir of water made by flooding a large area of land.

The dam's locks are 280m long and 35m wide.

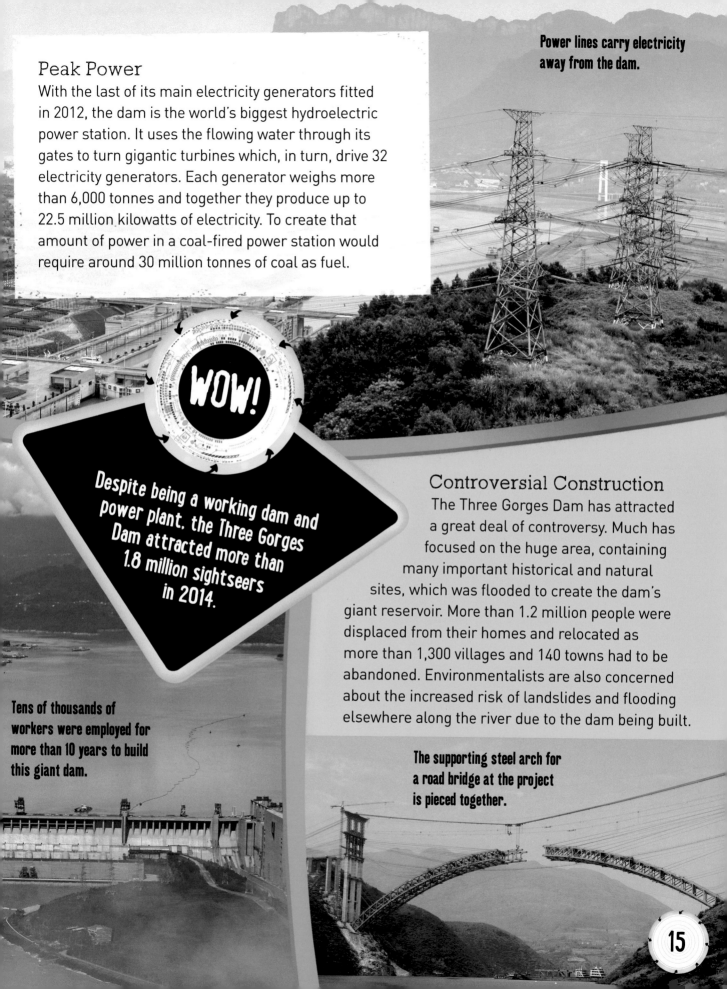

Peak Power

With the last of its main electricity generators fitted in 2012, the dam is the world's biggest hydroelectric power station. It uses the flowing water through its gates to turn gigantic turbines which, in turn, drive 32 electricity generators. Each generator weighs more than 6,000 tonnes and together they produce up to 22.5 million kilowatts of electricity. To create that amount of power in a coal-fired power station would require around 30 million tonnes of coal as fuel.

Power lines carry electricity away from the dam.

WOW!

Despite being a working dam and power plant, the Three Gorges Dam attracted more than 1.8 million sightseers in 2014.

Controversial Construction

The Three Gorges Dam has attracted a great deal of controversy. Much has focused on the huge area, containing many important historical and natural sites, which was flooded to create the dam's giant reservoir. More than 1.2 million people were displaced from their homes and relocated as more than 1,300 villages and 140 towns had to be abandoned. Environmentalists are also concerned about the increased risk of landslides and flooding elsewhere along the river due to the dam being built.

Tens of thousands of workers were employed for more than 10 years to build this giant dam.

The supporting steel arch for a road bridge at the project is pieced together.

Burj Khalifa

Welcome to the tallest building on the planet! The mighty Burj Khalifa is designed as the centrepiece of a development in Dubai, the biggest city in the United Arab Emirates. It contains a staggering 160 floors and soars more than 828m above the ground.

Building the Burj Khalifa

After 1,325 days of construction involving 12,000 workers at its peak, the building was opened in 2010. Its distinctive shape is based on the Hymenocallis, a local desert flower (left). It sits on a base made of steel and concrete with 192 piles extending to a depth of over 50m below ground. More than 31,000 tonnes of steel were used in its construction along with vast amounts of concrete. The resulting building weighs over 450,000 tonnes empty – about the same weight as 100,000 monster trucks!

The building's irregular shape helps to stop the tower swaying in high winds.

WOW!

Solar panels on the Burj Khalifa heat 140,000 litres of water each day. This is then circulated around the homes and offices in the building, saving around 3,200,000 watts of electricity per day.

Feature-Packed

The Burj Khalifa contains a multi-floor hotel, more than 900 apartments and underground parking for 3,000 vehicles. To give an idea of scale, even with the use of robotic window cleaners on the top levels, it takes over three months to clean all the building's 24,348 windows, which cover an area of 120,000 m². The water collected from the building's air-conditioning system each year would fill 20 Olympic-sized swimming pools and is used to water the landscaped gardens surrounding the building.

Window cleaners abseil down the lower floors of the building as they work.

Record-Breaker

The building's many records range from being the tallest structure ever built to having the world's highest nightclub (on its 144th floor). Its 76th floor features the highest swimming pool in the Middle East and the world's highest mosque is found on the 158th floor. Its 124th floor observation deck was the highest in the world until China's Canton Tower opened one higher. The Khalifa responded in 2014 with a new record-breaking observation area 555m above ground on the 148th floor.

The Panama Canal

A canal across the narrow land bridge of Central America had long been the dream of sailors and traders. The Panama Canal allowed passage between the Atlantic and Pacific Oceans without sailing around Cape Horn – the southernmost tip of South America. As a result, thousands of kilometres of sailing was slashed from voyages, saving time and money.

False Starts

Completion of the Suez Canal in Egypt, in 1869, spurred interest in creating a similar passage across Central America. In 1881 and 1894, the French made two attempts at canal building through Panama, but suffered financial disasters and the deaths of around 20,000 workers, mostly due to diseases such as malaria and yellow fever. Between 1904 and 1914, the United States took control. Workers overcame tough conditions and huge engineering challenges to complete the 80km canal.

In 2015, a staggering 13,874 ships and boats travelled through the Panama Canal.

At its peak, construction of the canal employed more than 45,000 workers.

CARIBBEAN SEA

COSTA RICA

PANAMA CANAL

PANAMA

COLOMBIA

NORTH PACIFIC OCEAN

Serious Shipping

The Panama Canal proved a resounding success. Thousands of vessels pass through its waters and locks every year and in September 2010, the *Fortune Plum* bulk carrier ship became the canal's one millionth vessel. In total, around three per cent of all the world's trade passes through the canal each year. Every ship pays a toll or fee based on its size, the amount of cargo it carries or the number of rooms and passengers it contains. In 2010, the *Norwegian Pearl* cruise ship paid the highest ever toll of US$375,600.

The Canal Expands

In 1999, control of the canal was passed to Panama, which now benefits from over US$1.5 billion of tolls every year. Between 2007 and 2016, over US$5 billion has been re-invested on expanding and improving the canal.

WOW!

Richard Halliburton swam through the Panama Canal in 1928. He paid its lowest recorded toll – just US$0.36!

Around 130 million cubic metres of soil and rock were removed as new, larger locks were built so that bigger container ships and cruise liners can use the canal.

The Eiffel Tower

Originally opened in 1889 as a temporary monument with a maximum life of 20 years, the Eiffel Tower celebrated its 125th birthday in 2014. The Iron Lady, as she is known, was built to commemorate 100 years since the French Revolution and at 300m high was the worlds tallest structure for 41 years. Today, the Eiffel Tower still dominates the Paris skyline and attracts almost seven million visitors every year.

Innovative Design

Gustave Eiffel was a prominent engineer and bridge builder who was invited to create a giant pylon or tower in the Champ de Mars park near the River Seine in the centre of Paris. Eiffel's clever design was sturdy and strong and left large enough spaces for winds to pass through. It involved more than 18,000 pieces of wrought iron, weighing more than 7,000 tonnes. These were assembled using tower cranes also designed by Eiffel. For a structure almost twice as high as the previous world's tallest – the Washington Monument – the Eiffel Tower was built fast. It was completed in less than 2 years, 3 months.

The tower's iron structure is held together by some 2.5 million rivets.

Tower Features

The Eiffel Tower begins with a giant 125m x 125m base which consists of four giant semi-circular arches. Rising above them are three floors or levels. Eiffel even built a small apartment on the third level which he used for entertaining friends and conducting weather experiments. The first and second levels house restaurants, gift shops and a museum, along with viewing areas. The names of 72 engineers, scientists and mathematicians who helped with the construction are engraved on the side of the tower.

Changes and Preservation

Over the years, the tower has been used as a weather station, a science lab for experiments and has had its lifts overhauled and replaced. In 2014, a glass floor was added to part of the first level. Since 2004 an ice rink has been built every winter on the first level as well. The tower has been repainted 18 times to protect its iron structure from rusting. Each repainting operation lasts more than a year and requires more than 50 tonnes of paint, 1,500 paintbrushes, 5,000 sanding discs and a team of 25 specialist painters to complete.

Some 20,000 light bulbs illuminate the Eiffel Tower each night.

WOW!

The tower's modern lifts travel a total combined distance of 103.000km a year – that's approximately two and a half times round the Earth.

The Bailong Elevator

Reaching a height of 326m, the Bailong Elevator (also known as the Hundred Dragons Elevator) is the tallest outdoor lift in the world. Unlike most lifts, which run inside a building or on its outside, the Bailong Elevator runs up the side of a rocky cliff face.

Visitors enjoy stunning views of the dramatic landscape that surrounds the Elevator.

Park Life

Zhangjiajie National Forest Park was China's first national forest park and became a UNESCO World Heritage site in 1992. The large park, found in Hunan Province, is famous for its natural beauty including spectacular rock stacks. One rock formation, known as 'Soldiers Gathering Together', could previously be viewed from the top of a quartz sandstone cliff only after an arduous trek lasting two hours or longer. The Bailong Elevator now takes less than two minutes to reach the top.

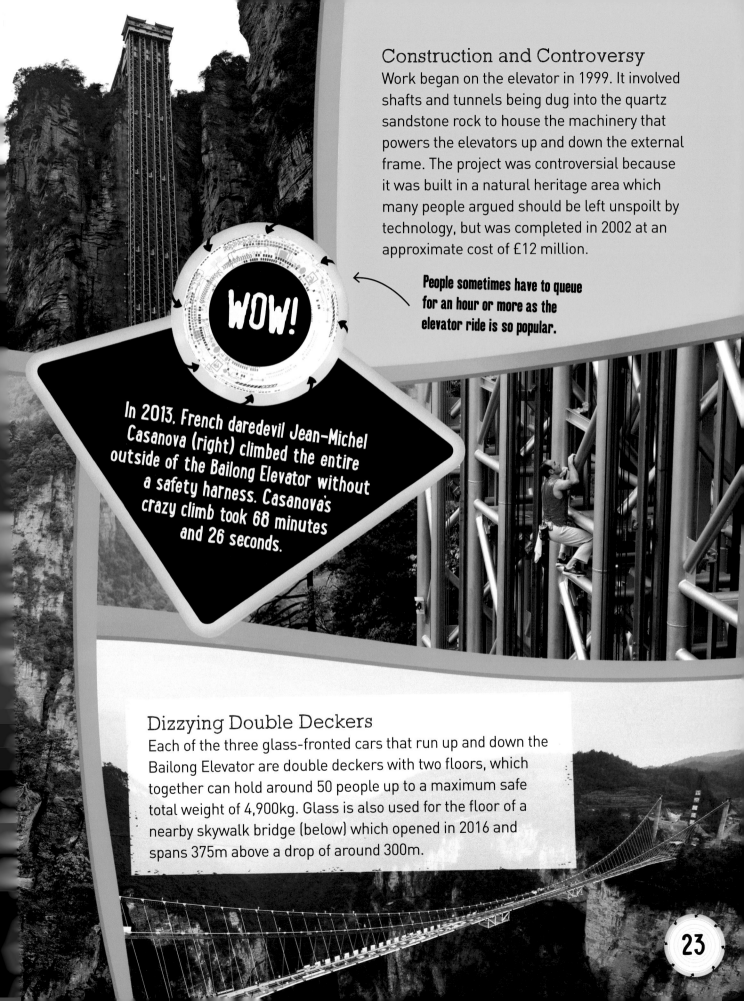

Construction and Controversy

Work began on the elevator in 1999. It involved shafts and tunnels being dug into the quartz sandstone rock to house the machinery that powers the elevators up and down the external frame. The project was controversial because it was built in a natural heritage area which many people argued should be left unspoilt by technology, but was completed in 2002 at an approximate cost of £12 million.

People sometimes have to queue for an hour or more as the elevator ride is so popular.

WOW!

In 2013, French daredevil Jean-Michel Casanova (right) climbed the entire outside of the Bailong Elevator without a safety harness. Casanova's crazy climb took 68 minutes and 26 seconds.

Dizzying Double Deckers

Each of the three glass-fronted cars that run up and down the Bailong Elevator are double deckers with two floors, which together can hold around 50 people up to a maximum safe total weight of 4,900kg. Glass is also used for the floor of a nearby skywalk bridge (below) which opened in 2016 and spans 375m above a drop of around 300m.

The Statue of Liberty

A gift from France to the United States, the Statue of Liberty or Liberty Enlightening the World stands on Liberty Island near the mouth of New York Harbor. The brainchild of French sculptor, Frédéric Auguste Bartholdi, the 46m-tall statue stands on a 47m-high pedestal.

The statue has a 10.67m waistline and 7.6m-long feet which are shrouded by the folds of her robes.

Built and Rebuilt

This famous landmark of New York was built not once but twice. It was first completed by Bartholdi in Paris in 1884, after more than a decade of hard work. It was then taken apart and packed into 214 crates for transport across the Atlantic Ocean by the French ship *Isère*. Surviving storms, *Isère* arrived in New York in October 1885 and was welcomed at the docks by 200,000 people. The statue was rebuilt and opened the following year.

In high winds, the torch held by the Statue of Liberty sways as much as 15cm from side to side.

The copper tarnished after years of exposure to the elements to form the green-tinted patina on the statue's surface.

Refurb and Preserve

In 1986, the statue's torch was replaced with a new model that featured a flame covered in a layer of 24 carat gold. The statue was also closed for a year from October 2011 to upgrade visitor facilities. In 2014, a staggering 4.2 million people visited Liberty Island, but only a handful went inside the statute. To help preserve its interior, just 240 people each day are allowed to climb the staircase inside to reach the crown at the top.

Copper Covered

Eiffel Tower builder, Gustave Eiffel designed the large internal frame. It contained 1,350 ribs and vertical posts, all made of iron, which reinforced the giant statue. Inside was a central pylon which anchored the statue to its large concrete pedestal and spiral staircases with more than 350 steps from the statue's base to its crown. Over the frame were placed 350 moulded sheets of copper, hand-beaten to a thickness of just 2.4mm. These form the outer surface of the statue and are fastened in place by 50mm-wide iron straps and some 300,000 copper rivets.

The Large Hadron Collider

Housed deep underground is the worlds most complex and high-tech set of physics experiments. The Large Hadron Collider (LHC) was built by CERN, the European Organization for Nuclear Research and first ran in 2008. It fires beams of tiny atomic particles called protons. These crash into one another at incredibly high speeds. The aim is to see what these collisions reveal about what the Universe is really made of and how it began.

A construction worker (bottom centre) stands in front of the giant ATLAS detector inside the Large Hadron Collider.

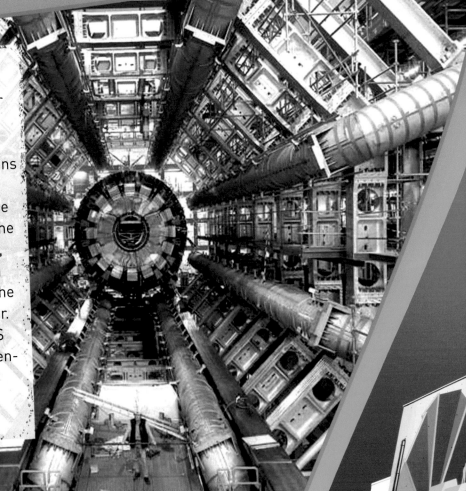

Going Underground

The LHC is a 27km-long circular tunnel constructed between 50 and 175m underground. It lies beneath the Jura Mountains on the border of France and Switzerland. More than a decade of work was required to equip the tunnel with all of its machinery, including giant detectors which measure what happens when the protons smash into one another. The largest of these, the ATLAS detector, is the height of a seven-storey building, weighs 7,000 tonnes and involved the work of 1,700 scientists.

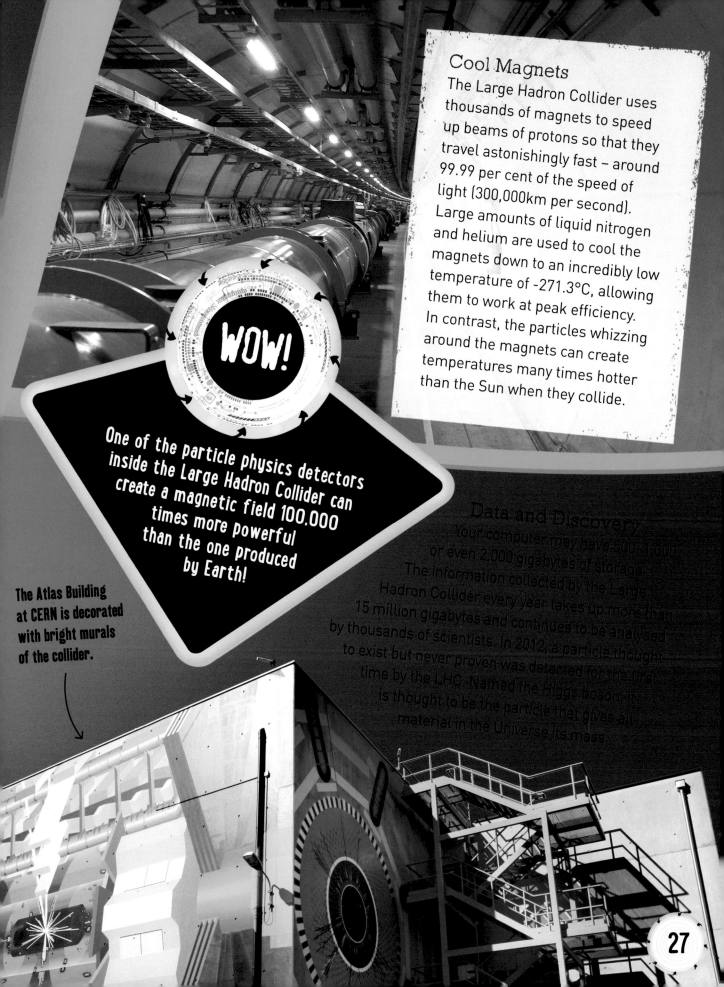

Cool Magnets

The Large Hadron Collider uses thousands of magnets to speed up beams of protons so that they travel astonishingly fast – around 99.99 per cent of the speed of light (300,000km per second). Large amounts of liquid nitrogen and helium are used to cool the magnets down to an incredibly low temperature of -271.3°C, allowing them to work at peak efficiency. In contrast, the particles whizzing around the magnets can create temperatures many times hotter than the Sun when they collide.

WOW!

One of the particle physics detectors inside the Large Hadron Collider can create a magnetic field 100,000 times more powerful than the one produced by Earth!

The Atlas Building at CERN is decorated with bright murals of the collider.

Data and Discovery

Your computer may have 500, 1,000, or even 2,000 gigabytes of storage. The information collected by the Large Hadron Collider every year takes up more than 15 million gigabytes and continues to be analysed by thousands of scientists. In 2012, a particle thought to exist but never proven was detected for the first time by the LHC. Named the Higgs boson, it is thought to be the particle that gives all material in the Universe its mass.

More Man-Made Wonders

All over the world there are astonishing buildings and structures that show people's ingenuity and their amazing design, engineering and construction abilities – from underground cathedrals of salt and history-making canals to towering statues and bridges.

The Wieliczka Salt Mine

Mining for salt for centuries at Wieliczka, near the Polish city of Krakow, has resulted in more than 200km of tunnels, caverns and chambers deep underground. Many chambers have been highly decorated with altars, sculptures and even chandeliers holding lights (right), all carved out of the rock salt formations. These eye-catching creations attract more than a million tourists every year.

The Golden Gate Bridge

The majestic Golden Gate Bridge spans San Francisco Bay. The 1,280m-long main span of this suspension bridge was the longest in the world when it opened in 1937. Both of its towers are made of steel fastened together by approximately 600,000 rivets. The road deck is suspended from giant cables, each of which is made from 27,572 strands of wire. In 1985, Dr Arthur Molinari became the billionth driver to cross the bridge. He received a case of champagne and a building site hard hat as a prize!

Christ the Redeemer

Towering over the Brazilian city of Rio de Janeiro, Cristo Redentor (Christ The Redeeemer in Brazilian Portuguese), is a 30m-tall statue of Jesus Christ made from reinforced concrete covered in soapstone. Built between 1923 and 1931 on the top of Corcovado, a 700m-high mountain, the statue is visited by around 5,000 people every day.

The statue overlooks the Hipódromo da Gávea horse-racing track, which opened in 1926.

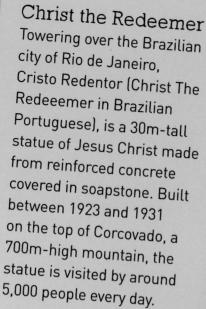

Suez Canal

Opened in 1869, the Suez Canal provided a massive 7,000km shortcut for shipping in the Mediterranean Sea bound for Asia or East Africa. The 193km-long canal runs through Egypt from the Mediterranean to the Red Sea and in 2014, 17,148 ships travelled along it. The following year, an extension to the canal opened, which featured a 35km-long second channel for bigger ships alongside the original canal to help cut waiting times.

Glossary and Further Information

commemorate
To remember or celebrate something in the past in some way, such as by holding a ceremony or building a monument.

controversy
A long and serious public debate or disagreement about a subject, such as the building of a new structure.

detours
Longer than usual routes taken to either avoid something such as roadworks or to visit somewhere along the way.

displaced
Describes something that has been moved from its usual or normal position. In human geography, it describes people who have been forced to move from their homes to live elsewhere.

excavate
To dig and remove earth and rocks or to dig carefully to try to find ancient objects at an archaeological site.

foundations
The lowest part of a building or structure, usually below ground, which must bear the weight of the rest of the structure.

hydroelectric power
Electricity generated by moving or falling water turning devices called turbines which power an electricity generator.

lock
A device, usually on a section of a river or canal, which is closed off by gates, allowing ships to be raised or lowered when travelling between different stretches of water.

mass
A measure of how matter there is in an object.

patina
A film of material on the surface of copper, bronze or some other metals, usually caused by chemical reactions with the oxygen in air.

piles
Long, slender columns driven into the ground and used to support a heavy load of a building, road or other structure.

storey
A complete floor or level of a building.

tarnished
When the shiny surface of a metal becomes dull.

tonne
A unit of weight equal to 1,000kg.

viaduct
A type of bridge consisting of arches or spans that carry a road or rail line across a wide valley.

Books

The Land and the People: India
by Susie Brooks (Wayland, 2016)

Visual Explorers: Wonders of the World
by Paul Calver and Toby Reynolds
(Franklin Watts, 2016)

Unpacked: Poland by Clive Gifford (Wayland, 2015)

Unpacked: China by Susie Brooks (Wayland, 2015)

Websites

https://www.youtube.com/watch?v=mMli3N7yjgA
Watch this short video of time lapse photos showing how the Burj Khalifa was constructed.

http://www.technologystudent.com/culture1/empire1.htm
Learn more about the techniques that were used to erect the Empire State Building so quickly.

http://www.nps.gov/featurecontent/stli/eTour.htm
Take an official tour of the Statue of Liberty from your computer with this webpage from the US National Parks Service.

http://www.toureiffel.paris/en/everything-about-the-tower/themed-files.html
These themed webpages about different aspects of the Eiffel Tower add up to a complete guide about the structure.

https://www.sydneyoperahouse.com/our-story.html
Grab lots of facts about the Sydney Opera House.

https://www.pancanal.com/eng/general/howitworks/index.html
Watch three animations of the Panama Canals scale, how it works and how ships travel through its locks at the official canal website.

http://english.alarabiya.net/en/perspective/features/2015/08/05/A-look-at-Egypt-s-Suez-Canal-past-and-present.html
Check out this fun and informative inforgraphic on the Suez Canal, its route, and its importance for world trade.

Index